T0369949

# COUNT
# DOWN

*Countdown* is excerpted from *End Times Made Easy*, written by Joseph Morris and published by Harrison House in 2022.

Published by Harrison House Publishers
Shippensburg, PA 17257

ISBN 13 TP: 978-1-6675-0758-3
ISBN 13 eBook: 978-1-6675-0759-0

For Worldwide Distribution, Printed in the U.S.A.
1 2 3 4 5 6 7 8 / 29 28 27 26 25

# COUNT DOWN

### PROPHETIC TIMELINES
### OF THE RAPTURE AND
### JESUS' SECOND COMING

## JOSEPH MORRIS

# CONTENTS

# FOREWORD

It's almost midnight prophetically!

Not long after I was born again, I had a dream that transformed my life. In the dream, I was standing in a field close to my childhood home. The place was crowded with people chatting and having a great time.

Abruptly, a noise unlike anything I had ever heard broke through the casual conversations. It seemed as though the heavens were singing. I looked up and saw a massive clock appearing through the clouds. It had large Roman numerals, and both hands of the clock were nearly pointing straight up. It was almost midnight.

I looked around to see if anyone else had noticed, but it seemed like only a handful did. The others carried on with their day, completely unaware of the magnificent spectacle above them. When I recognized what was going on, my heart began to race because I knew what this meant.

I felt something strange take hold of me as the second hand got closer to the 12. I started to rise up, feet lifting off the floor, like metal being slowly pulled to a magnet. One of my friends saw what was happening and tried to join me by reaching out. However, it was already too late. It was now midnight, and he wasn't ready. His hands reached for the sky, but he stayed on the ground, a desperate expression on his face.

And then I woke up with the words, "Jesus is coming," on my lips. And now, decades later, still echoing in my spirit are those three simple words. They serve as a heavenly reminder of how urgent the hour is.

That dream was my wake-up call, but this book is yours.

Joseph Morris has written *Countdown* with a laser-sharp focus on the final moments before Jesus' return, and if there's one thing I can tell you, it's this: the clock is ticking. This isn't about wild speculation, but about understanding the prophetic word that God has given for this hour.

When you read this book, you'll learn that we are not living in a time of uncertainty. For believers, there's no guessing game when it comes to where we are on God's prophetic calendar. Everything is falling into place just as He said it would. And here's the thrilling part—God is letting us be part of this story! As Joseph writes, "The countdown has begun," and it's time to wake up, pick up the pace, and accelerate toward the finish line.

Throughout these pages, you'll find a balance of deep scriptural teaching and practical encouragement that will inspire you to get ready for what's coming next: the Rapture. As Brother Morris often says, it isn't an escape for the fearful, but an evacuation for the faithful. The Bride of Christ is about to be whisked away to meet her Bridegroom, and we have a role to play in the days leading up to that glorious event.

What I appreciate most about Joseph's approach is his heart. This book isn't written to scare you or confuse you—it's here to comfort and energize you. Like Jesus' parable of the wise and foolish virgins, the message is simple: Get your lamps filled with oil. Get ready. Be expectant. Because whether you're aware of it or not, you've been chosen for such a time as this.

God's prophetic plan is unfolding before our very eyes.

I've seen a lot of folks either dismiss the topic of the end times or treat it like a mysterious puzzle no one can figure out. That ends now. With clarity and passion, Joseph Morris connects the dots in a way that will have you nodding your head in agreement and wanting to shout from the rooftops: "Jesus is coming!"

*Countdown* is not a book to read passively. It's a wake-up call, a trumpet blast. As Joseph reminds us, this is not the time to coast into the finish. We're in a relay race, and we've been handed the baton at the most crucial stage. So, as you read this book, ask yourself, "Am I running like I believe the King is coming?" Because He is. And I promise you, nothing will matter more when that trumpet sounds.

Now, let's dive in together—because the countdown has already begun.

Alan DiDio
Host of *Encounter Today*

## INTRODUCTION

# THE COUNTDOWN HAS BEGUN!

The stage is set—2,700 years in the making—and we are witnessing the final signs fall into place before we see Jesus Christ face to face. But countdowns don't last long, and time is running out as the end of the age approaches.

The next event for believers on God's prophetic calendar is upon us: the Rapture. It's not an escape for believers but an evacuation. The Church will leave the chaos and turmoil of this world to attend a private coronation ceremony and celebration. When you understand the appointment already marked on your calendar, you will want to obey God like never before to accelerate His return!

But the Rapture is just the beginning. Jesus' Second Coming is the granddaddy of all events throughout the universe and all eternity. It's the moment when the King of kings will be honored on this earth. Like the hero arriving in the final act of a great movie, every knee will bow, and we will witness the grand and public coronation of King Jesus, with all the pomp and circumstance due Him. This will be the ultimate, over-the-top, glorious climax of history, where the entire world will acknowledge Jesus as the rightful ruler of all.

Don't just watch from the sidelines—*get ready!* Dive into the scriptural explanations on the pages that follow to understand exactly what the Bible says about these end-time events and their timing. The countdown clock is ticking, and it's time for the Church to hustle! It's time for us to do the works of Jesus and get ready to meet our King.

—Joe Morris

# CHAPTER 1

# JESUS APPEARED TO ME WITH AN END-TIME MANDATE

Everywhere you turn there are signs that Jesus is coming soon. You can easily look around today and picture your future because blatant signs are found in Bible prophecy and news headlines. It's very intentional. Jesus is trying to show you how near we are to His return. He does not want these signs to frighten you, but He does want them to wake you up. He wants you to recognize the hour you are living in.

Jesus wants these end-time signs to make you bold and motivate you to pick up your pace and accelerate doing the will of God. The more intimately you get to know Jesus and what His Word says about His return, the freer and more excited you will be.

But there is something else Jesus wants you to know more than anything else: He wants you to know how much He loves you and how excited He is to see you face to face.

On more than one occasion, Jesus has appeared to me with a mandate to preach on His return. In 1987, Jesus appeared to me and told me to preach on end times. Respectfully, I explained that I did not want to preach on that topic.

> On more than one occasion, Jesus has appeared to me with a mandate to preach on His return.

"But, Lord," I said, "I don't want to be weird. People equate end times with weirdness. You know, it's right up there with locust burgers and weird hair—just strange."

"This is what I want you to do," Jesus said. "It's what you're supposed to do."

Four years later in 1990, Jesus appeared to me again. At first, He just looked at me because I had not preached on end times like He told me to do. At the time, I was staying in Michigan at Tom and Judy Hicks' house preparing for a service that night. I was praying in their really cool office. The den had walnut walls and an amazing fireplace. Sandi Patti music was playing, and I was praying in tongues, getting ready to go preach.

All of a sudden, the presence of God filled the room, and I began to cry. I thought, *Lord, You are so good to me! Why are You so good to me?* I looked up, and there was Jesus, leaning against the desk in front of me. He was wearing a white robe with an olive-green sash, and His hands were folded behind His back.

I was no longer crying at that point; I was outright bawling. Jesus just looked at me. I was overcome by His presence and crying uncontrollably because of the goodness coming out of Him.

Jesus continued looking at me. I knew that He had come because I hadn't preached what He wanted me to preach. He could have said, "Hey, you're a loser. You haven't done what you're supposed to do." But He just sat there and looked

at me, and His goodness led me to repentance
(2 Pet. 3:15).

I realize now the urgency of His end-time
mandate. Why is it so urgent? Because Jesus wants
you prepared and loved. The number-one thing
Jesus really instructed me to tell you is how much
He loves you. Friend, no matter how much you
already believe Jesus loves you, that number can be
magnified by a billion trillion. In fact, you could
not magnify it enough to show you just how much
He adores you. Jesus cares deeply for you and
wants you nourished, instructed, and strengthened.
He only wants good things for you, and He gave
His life to prove it.

> Friend, no matter how much you
> already believe Jesus loves you, that
> number can be magnified by a
> billion trillion.

God has gotten blamed for so many evil things
the devil does, but the Bible says every good gift
and every perfect gift is from above, and that never

changes (James 1:17). Your Father loves you and wants you excited, hopeful, and happy when Jesus raptures the Church. He wants you so happy that you are almost giddy. People may even think there's something wrong with you and ask, "Why are you so happy anyway?"

You will answer, "Because I'm about to see Jesus Christ, my Savior and Lord, face to face!"

I absolutely light up when my phone rings and I see a picture of my only daughter calling who lives several states away. I drop everything to talk to my little girl. She is a married woman now with a child of her own, but she will always still be my little girl. And, if I think like that, imagine how Jesus thinks about you. He can't wait to see you in person, and we should have a radical joy about seeing Him face to face.

Jesus wants us to finish our courses on earth with joy because joy is our strength (Neh. 8:10), and He knows we need strength to finish strong. He wants the message of His soon return pumped into us, enabling us to run faster and get more accomplished in a shorter period of time. We have been destined to close off the Church Age, and we have more to get done than any generation before us.

Think about it. You are about to be caught up to meet Jesus in the air. How cool is that? This King we worship and serve will go from faith to sight. You will see His eyes that are flames of fire and His feet of fine brass. You will see the love in His eyes and the nail prints in His hands. And in heaven, you will see the fountain filled with blood, drawn from Emmanuel's veins.

Yet before that day, we have a lot of inheritance to walk in. We have a lot of important things to do in this hour to accomplish the will of God and prepare for His coming. God's agenda in this hour is to love you, inform you, bless you, strengthen you, and help you because there's destiny on you just as there is on America and every nation.

From the very beginning of this nation more than 245 years ago, I believe Christians walked this continent praying and decreeing God's will over this nation and what would happen right before the coming of the Lord. We are all walking out those prayers even now, so let's be faithful to fulfill

them and get the message of Jesus to everyone—
next door and from coast to coast. You and I need
to daily demonstrate that Jesus came out of the
grave.

There's just so much happening right now.
You are living at a time when all of the prophetic
verses in the Bible are coming to pass. I remember end-time preachers 20 to 30 years ago who
would lay out everything that had to happen—all
the pieces of the puzzle that would need to fall in
place and come together before Jesus could return.
But, my friend, we are there! Last week something
happened that was a sign of His coming. The
week before that something happened. Yesterday
something happened. Literally, the dots are con-
necting before your eyes with Bible verses coming
to pass click, click, click. It's an exciting time, a
rejoicing time!

> You are living at a time when all of
> the prophetic verses in the Bible are
> coming to pass.

# TIME TO ACCELERATE

As you begin to recognize the timing of Jesus' return and the signs all around, it will propel you in your race. It will fuel you to run faster. After all, when you're running a race, you don't slow down when you can see the finish line. You run faster—a whole lot faster! That what Jesus wants you to do now.

My daughter ran cross-country in high school, and I remember how she practiced hard for every race. Every day she ran miles and miles, and I did my best to cheer her on. I would get on my motorcycle and ride beside her, shouting, "You're doing good, Lauren! You're doing great! Keep going!" She would run four or five miles and not even be tired, while I got tired just riding my motorcycle. On the weekends, Lauren would train even more intensely for her cross-country events.

I'm so glad I got to attend almost every single race because I loved cheering for her. I would be right there at the first mile marker waiting for her, and she would come running by yelling out, "Daddy, how far? How far?"

"Lauren, you've got two more miles. Pace yourself!" I would answer. She asked about the distance because she was calculating how much energy she should exert at that point.

I didn't want her to give it all out at the beginning, so I'd say, "Pace yourself, Lauren! Two more miles!"

Then I would cut across the field to beat her to the next mile marker. The first thing she would say when she would run up is, "Daddy, how far? How far now?"

"Lauren, you've got another mile," I would answer. "Pace yourself! You've got plenty of time!"

Eventually, there would come a point in the race where I would cut over to the last place, and as she would come running up to reach that marker, she would see the finish line. She would see me but not say a word to me at that point. She no longer asked, "Hey, Daddy, how far? How far?" No, she could see the finish line for herself.

Her countenance would change. Joy would come all over her. All that practice, all that training, all that hard work every day meant nothing until, all of a sudden, right there I could see determination all over her face.

She was saying to herself, "I'm not going to come to the end of this race and slow down now. Let's blow it out!"

I would scream, *"RUN!"* And everything about her changed. I could see it on her face and in her movement. She picked up her pace, resolute to finish the race.

Words were not necessary, but I would scream just the same, "RUN! RUN, LAUREN, *RUN!* The finish line is just ahead! *GO!"* And she would cross that line and finish with her hand in the air—victory all over her!

My friend, *you* are also in a race—the race of your life! We all are. Can you see the finish line just ahead? It's the finish line for the Church Age. And it's time to RUN! RUN, CHURCH, *RUN!* The finish line is just ahead! *Go!* It's time to finish with your hand in the air—victory all over you!

> It's time to RUN! RUN, CHURCH, *RUN!* The finish line is just ahead! *Go!*

In a relay race, the fastest guys always run at the end. That means the Lord looked down through the corridors of time and picked you to run fast at the end. He is right now giving you a heightened awareness about these last of the last days.

Everything we've been taught until now has been an investment of the Word for our generation, and it's time to accelerate. Jesus is calling on those investments now. He's tapping all those spiritual deposits right now. Greater is He that is in you than he that is in this world (Jn. 4:4). Whatsoever is born of God overcomes the world. This is the victory that overcomes the world, even our faith (1 Jn. 5:4). Come on now!

# PROPHECY TO THIS GENERATION

There is something in you that no other generation has ever had. Daniel saw you and prophesied about you. He said you would be strong. He said you would know your God and do exploits! (See Daniel 11:32.) Okay, it's time. That day has come.

A lot of people know the Word of God, but not the God of the Word. I believe God is getting us acquainted with the God of the Word so we can step into our end-time destiny.

This is a time like no other. We are privileged to watch verse after verse after verse come to pass. There are more verses about the time we live in right now and the Tribulation period than any other topic in the Bible. In fact, the Bible is one-third prophecy, so, clearly, this topic is on God's heart, and there's more documentation right in front of us than ever before.

So, let's get into what the Bible has to say about end times. These verses will comfort us, excite us, strengthen us, and help us pick up the pace so we can run our race and cross the finish line.

# CHAPTER 2

# THE RAPTURE

Take a good look at your body and remember what it looks like because it won't be long before your mortal body will put on immortality. Death will be swallowed up in life and, at last, you will lose the stain of Adam. You will have a brand-new glorified body that never dies, never gets sick, never ages, walks through walls, and instantly translates from heaven to earth. Your earth suit with its sin nature of Adam will become only a distant memory. It's going to be wonderful!

For the most part, the Rapture is not talked about in the Gospels, but we do find one shadow of reference to the Rapture in John 14. It's pretty powerful!

# WILL YOU MARRY ME?

Actually, this split-second reference to the Rapture in the Gospel of John is an extreme statement. Basically, Jesus asked His disciples to marry Him.

### JOHN 14:1-3
*Let not your heart be troubled: ye believe in God, believe also in me. In my Father's house are many mansions: if it were not so, I would have told you. I go to prepare a place for you. And if I go and prepare a place for you, I will come again, and receive you unto myself; that where I am, there ye may be also.*

This was a Jewish wedding proposal. I can just imagine Jesus' staff—Peter, James, and John—saying, "Whoa, whoa, whoa! *What?*" They were just normal guys, but there was nothing normal about this proposal. Jesus freaked them out! It would have freaked me out, but as you know, Jesus often said interesting things just like that to get people's attention and prepare them for what was to come.

Think about it. Jesus walked up to His staff and said, "Oh, by the way, will you guys marry Me?" They were like, "Uh, hold on. Guys don't ask guys to marry them. Jesus has been out in the sun too long. Something is up here. Jesus says some interesting stuff, but this is, 'Will you marry me?'"

In the Jewish wedding tradition, a man would ask a woman to marry him and then pay the purchase price for her. In other words, there would be a redemption, and she would be set apart for the marriage. In the same way, Jesus paid the price of redemption for the Church with His own life and blood. And now we—the Church—have been set apart waiting for the Rapture.

According to tradition, the groom would go to his father's house and ask to marry the daughter. Upon his agreement, the father would then set about building a honeymoon suite for the couple, but the son would not know when the suite would be finished. Jewish tradition tells us the average wait time was about a year for the father to complete the wedding chamber or house.

Then, one day, the father would say to his son, "Okay, your room is ready! Go get your bride." During the time the room was built, the bride was to be continually preparing for her groom to come for her. She was to be ready and waiting!

People think, *Well, you can't know when the bridegroom is coming back.* Not so! That's just plain wrong teaching. Brides knew almost to the day when the bridegroom was returning, and they were anxiously waiting!

How many of you who are married knew when your wedding would take place? Did it catch you by surprise? No. Many people even send out "save the date" announcements. When our daughter, Lauren, got married, she had nine bridesmaids fly to California, and I've never worked so hard in all my life. Lauren said, "Hey, you will be able to do this, Dad. It's no big deal." I tell you what, nothing about her wedding caught me by surprise. I worked 24/7 just trying to get all the stuff done for the ceremony.

Yet when it comes to the Rapture, most people think it will be a surprise. Sure, the Rapture will be a surprise for the world, but it should not be a surprise for the bride—the Church. The bride of Christ should be expectant, ready, and anxiously waiting!

> Sure, the Rapture will be a surprise for the world, but it should not be a surprise for the bride—the Church.

The apostle Paul said, "But you aren't in the dark about these things, dear brothers and sisters, and you won't be surprised when the day of the Lord comes like a thief" (1 Thess. 5:4 NLT).

Jewish tradition specified that after the purchase price was paid, the bride would be set apart or sanctified. She would prepare herself as she got closer to the wedding date. Meanwhile, I've interviewed families in Israel who explained that how soon the groom returned for the bride was all based on money. If the family had a little bit of money, it would be like a tenth of a honeymoon chamber and take a while to build. If they had a lot of money, an elaborate room would be built quickly. The father would decide, *This is how much money I will spend on your room.* But it would almost always be about a year regardless of the money involved. Clearly, no one was clueless. The groom was preparing, and the bride was preparing.

Unfortunately, the Church has taught that no one can tell when Jesus is coming back. But the truth is, you *can* tell! Once you get into the Scriptures, it really becomes quite clear.

A Jewish father would tell his son, "I've got your room ready. Go get your bride!" The groom would run down with a shout and get his bride who had been getting herself ready. She would be preparing day by day with her ears perked up so she could run to meet him. Church, we, too, should have our ears perked up and be ready to run to meet our Groom. At the Rapture of the Church, Jesus will come down for us with a shout, and we will meet Him in the air, so shall we ever be with the Lord. Come on, folks!

Like we said earlier, our mortality will put on immortality. Hallelujah! For us that means we are never to get tired again, never to get sick again, never to gain weight again. (By the way, my weight is flawless. I just need to be 6 feet 3 inches. I'm the perfect weight for that height.) Praise God, everything will get corrected when we are quickened by His Spirit. Our cells will be quickened, and we will get a brand-new body. Aren't you looking forward to that day?

# WHAT PAUL SAYS ABOUT THE RAPTURE

In 1 Thessalonians, the first letter written by Paul, the theme of his writing is the coming of the Lord. In fact, Paul wrote the letter because the Thessalonians thought they were in the Tribulation. They were under so much persecution that Paul had to speak up, saying, "Hey, whoa, folks. Let me address some issues here!"

The Thessalonians had been taught the immediacy of the return of the Lord to the point that they were saying, "Something is wrong here! People are dying and going home to be with the Lord. What's up? I thought Jesus was going to come back before that?" Paul wrote them a letter saying, "Don't worry. Everything is cool."

As you read what Paul wrote about the Rapture, notice his tone and keep it in mind. Paul wants you hopeful and happy with no sorrow because that's the way Jesus wants you.

1 THESSALONIANS 4:13-18

*But I would not have you to be ignorant, brethren, concerning them which are asleep, that ye sorrow not, even as others which have no hope. For if we believe that Jesus died and rose again, even so them also which sleep in Jesus will God bring with him. For this we say unto you by the word of the Lord, that we which are alive and remain unto the coming of the Lord shall not prevent them which are asleep. For the Lord himself shall descend from heaven with a shout, with the voice of the archangel, and with the trump of God: and the dead in Christ shall rise first: then we which are alive and remain shall be caught up together with them in the clouds, to meet the Lord in the air: and so shall we ever be with the Lord. Wherefore comfort one another with these words.*

Let's read the same passage from the New Living Translation in more modern language:

*And now, dear brothers and sisters, we want you to know what will happen to the believers who have died so you will not grieve like people who have no hope. For since we believe that Jesus died and was raised to life again, we also believe that when Jesus returns, God will bring back with him the believers who have died. We tell you this directly from the Lord: We who are still living when the Lord returns will not meet him ahead of those who have died. For the Lord himself will come down from heaven with a commanding shout, with the voice of the archangel, and with the trumpet call of God. First, the believers who have died will rise from their graves. Then, together with them, we who are still alive and remain on the earth will be caught up in the clouds to meet the Lord in the air. Then we will be with the Lord forever. So encourage each other with these words.*

Does the last verse say we should scare one another with these words? No. The teaching of the Rapture is to bring comfort, so encourage each other. This is good news! As we've said before, there is bad news ahead— but not for the Christian. In fact, the King James Version says "comfort one another with these words." The New Living Translation says "encourage each other with these words," and in the margin of most Bibles, it says *exhort* one another with these words. This is our glorious hope! There should be a joy in the Church that we are about to be caught up. We are about to see Jesus face to face!

What generation will be here when the Rapture happens? Your generation, this generation. When you go through all the signs and do the math however you want to do it, it's still you. "Hey, Joe," somebody asks, "Can you really be that bold about Jesus' return?" You can if you can read.

"Hey, Joe," somebody asks, "Can you really be that bold about Jesus' return?" You can if you can read.

People confront me daily saying, "You cannot tell when the Lord is coming back." Yet Jesus had a whole tribe in the Old Testament called the Tribe of Issachar. First Chronicles 12:32 says they were "men that had understanding of the times, to know what Israel ought to do." The scripture indicates if you know what time it is, you know what to do. On the other hand, if you don't recognize the time, you won't know what you're supposed to do or recognize there is a change coming.

I've heard people say, "The Rapture is simply a doctrine of the Church that surfaced in the late 1800s." No. It came from right here in the Bible. It started with Jesus giving His disciples a wedding proposal. It came when Paul said to the Thessalonians, "Don't worry. Jesus will come back with a shout, and the dead in Christ will rise first."

*The Message* quotes 1 Thessalonians 4:15-18 this way:

> *We can tell you with complete confidence—*
> *we have the Master's word on it—that when*
> *the Master comes again to get us, those of us*
> *who are still alive will not get a jump on the*

*dead and leave them behind. In actual fact, they'll be ahead of us. The Master himself will give the command. Archangel thunder! God's trumpet blast! He'll come down from heaven and the dead in Christ will rise— they'll go first. Then the rest of us who are still alive at the time will be caught up with them into the clouds to meet the Master. Oh, we'll be walking on air! And then there will be one huge family reunion with the Master. So reassure one another with these words.*

Isn't this something? Every loved one who has gone on to be with the Lord will instantaneously be reunited with their flesh. Their molecules will recollect; their spirits will rejoin their bodies, and you will meet them in the air. What a reunion!

Jesus will say, "Come up hither!" and every one of those bodies will be completely remade at the same exact second your body is remade. Hallelujah! People ask, "Can the Lord heal me?" He already healed you 2,000 years ago, but Jesus will change your whole molecular structure with the shout of the archangel, the trumpet of God.

Woohoo! Together, we will rocket right out of the earth to meet Jesus in the air.

> Jesus will change your whole molecular structure with the shout of the archangel, the trumpet of God. Woohoo! Together, we will rocket right out of the earth to meet Jesus in the air.

Do you remember seeing pictures in old movies where the graves burst open at the Rapture? Not so—the graves will not burst open. Men and women will come right through their caskets just like you will go right through the ceiling. Nothing will contain you! When Jesus says, "Come up hither!" every born-again person on the planet will go north. Wow! Hallelujah! Talk about an evacuation!

No matter the country, when an army prepares to go into battle, the ambassadors are always evacuated first. God is also coming back for His ambassadors—and that's *you*.

# RAPTURE QUALIFICATIONS

In 1 Thessalonians 4:14, Paul listed the qualifications for going up in the Rapture.

> *For if we believe that Jesus died and rose again, even so them also which sleep in Jesus will God bring with him.*

As I travel and speak on end times, I hear a lot of frustrated people comment on this verse. I hear people say, "If you're perfect, you will go up in the Rapture. If you're not perfect, you will not go up in the Rapture." The truth is, if you are born again, you will go up. Friend, it's not about you— it's about Jesus coming for His body.

I want to be clear about this: You are either born again or you're not. There is no in-between. It's true that you cannot be a great, mature, and powerful Christian if you are carnal and living like the world, but you are still a Christian. You may not be doing what you should do, but that does not mean you lose your reborn nature; it does mean you are yielding to your carnal, fleshly nature.

There's a whole teaching right now that says if people don't believe in the Rapture or don't have faith for the Rapture, they won't go up in the Rapture. That's not biblical. Too many Christians have made it about "me." They ask, "Am I cool enough, good enough, godly enough, holy enough to go in the Rapture?" Yes, you are holy enough because Jesus made you holy (1 Cor. 1:30). Jesus made you the righteousness of God in Him (2 Cor. 5:21).

I've heard people ask, "What if the Rapture occurs, and I'm not doing everything I should be doing and doing some stuff I shouldn't be doing?" Listen, folks, I'm not giving you a license to sin; people will sin without a license. But I am telling you that Jesus purchased you and that qualifies you for the Rapture.

I travel ministering in churches all the time, and I'm asked all kinds of questions about this: "I drank the wrong cup of coffee, will I still go in the Rapture? I had some thoughts I shouldn't have, what will happen to me? I did some things I'm not proud of, am I qualified?" Listen—there is no bad strain of Jesus' blood. If you accepted Jesus as your Lord and Savior, then His blood washed you clean.

While I was preaching in Galveston, Texas, an angry lady walked up to me and said, "How dare you say if you're born again, you're going up in the Rapture." I thoroughly explained salvation to her—that it's not by works but by faith and grace. The Holy Ghost loves to magnify Jesus, and this is what He said to me about that lady: "Ask her whose works she would rather trust in—Mine or hers." Hebrews 1:3-4 says, "…when he had by himself purged our sins, sat down on the right hand of the Majesty on high: being made so much better than the angels, as he hath by inheritance obtained a more excellent name than they." All by Himself, Jesus redeemed you, and Hebrews makes the point over and over again.

I'm stressing this point because I want you to have joy about the Rapture. All the time, I hear people confess their biggest fear is whether or not they will go up in the Rapture. So, let me ask: are you saved? If you answer yes, then you're going up. If answer no, let's fix that now. Turn to page 114 and pray to receive Jesus as your Savior.

If you are born again, it's crazy to doubt you will go up in the Rapture. If I had only one leg and hopped everywhere I went, I would really look forward to receiving my other leg. It would be so wonderful to reunite with my leg. I'm sure you agree that sounds ridiculous. Likewise, Jesus is looking forward to rejoining His entire body—both legs and all the rest. Again, we've made salvation about us—am I cool enough, am I sharp enough. It does not matter—you are born again.

It's important to look at the Greek translation of these words. At the Rapture, there's an examination that's made, and the same word *examination* is used in reference to the Second Coming. At the Rapture of the Church, the righteous go up to meet Him in the air. At the Second Coming, the wicked are plucked off the earth, but both scriptures say "he makes an examination." You're either lit or not lit. There's no in-between. I know it makes religious people mad, but that's too bad. God's Word is the final authority.

If you are a Christian, Jesus has redeemed you. Period. The Rapture should produce zero fear for you. You don't need to earn your way to heaven or make your way there—Jesus already made the way. Come on! Jesus purchased you with His own blood. How dare anyone say His blood was not perfect enough to wash away sin.

> If you are a Christian, Jesus has redeemed you. Period. The Rapture should produce zero fear for you.

Hebrews 1:3 says by Himself Jesus purged our sins, so how dare we question if the blood is powerful enough to cleanse. "With his own blood—not the blood of goats and calves—he [Jesus] entered the Most Holy Place once for all time and secured our redemption forever" (Heb. 9:12 NLT). The Contemporary English Version says, "Then Christ went once for all into the most holy place and freed us from sin forever. He did this by offering his own blood instead of the blood of goats and bulls."

When the trumpet sounds at the Rapture and, all of a sudden, Jesus says, "Come up hither! Come up to the throne of God!" every born-again Christian will rock a brand-new body to heaven. Talk about a bright future! Your social calendar is already full. You have the Reward Seat of Christ to attend and the Marriage Supper of the Lamb. You have appointments with God, and you are living right before it all takes place.

Friend, live holy, and don't be stupid! It's no time to be acting like the devil. That would be idiotic. Why would you want to be wearing a spotted garment when you're about to meet Jesus in the air?

What would you think if I wore a sports jacket, took it off to dip it in the mud, and then put it on again? Wouldn't that be ridiculous? Who wants to wear a dirty garment? Or let's say you have two dresses in your closet, but one was ruined in the mud. Would you ever be torn about which one to wear? No. At the Rapture of the Church, Jesus will "subdue all things unto himself" (Phil. 3:21). The entire verse reads, "He will take our weak mortal bodies and change them into glorious bodies like his own, using the same power with which he will bring everything under his control" (NLT).

# A BODY RETROFITTED FOR GLORY

In Luke 24, Jesus gives you some insight about the new body you will receive when you meet Him in the sky. Very early on Sunday morning the women who went to Jesus' tomb with spices found the stone had been rolled away from the entrance. Two angels told the women that Jesus had been raised from the dead. Later that same day, Jesus appeared to two men on the road to Emmaus as they were talking about all that had happened.

## LUKE 24:15-24 (NLT)

*As they talked and discussed these things, Jesus himself suddenly came and began walking with them. But God kept them from recognizing him. He asked them, "What are you discussing so intently as you walk along?" They stopped short, sadness written*

*across their faces. Then one of them, Cleopas, replied, "You must be the only person in Jerusalem who hasn't heard about all the things that have happened there the last few days."*
*"What things?" Jesus asked. "The things that happened to Jesus, the man from Nazareth," they said. "He was a prophet who did powerful miracles, and he was a mighty teacher in the eyes of God and all the people. But our leading priests and other religious leaders handed him over to be condemned to death, and they crucified him. We had hoped he was the Messiah who had come to rescue Israel. This all happened three days ago. Then some women from our group of his followers were at his tomb early this morning, and they came back with an amazing report. They said his body was missing, and they had seen angels who told them Jesus is alive! Some of our men ran out to see, and sure enough, his body was gone, just as the women had said."*

Jesus had some pretty straight words for the two men:

## LUKE 24:25-27 (NLT)

*Then Jesus said to them, "You foolish people! You find it so hard to believe all that the prophets wrote in the Scriptures. Wasn't it clearly predicted that the Messiah would have to suffer all these things before entering his glory?" Then Jesus took them through the writings of Moses and all the prophets, explaining from all the Scriptures the things concerning himself.*

As the men were nearing Emmaus and the end of their journey, Jesus acted as if He was going on. But they begged Him to stay since it was late:

## LUKE 24:29-35 (NLT)

*…So he [Jesus] went home with them. As they sat down to eat, he took the bread and blessed it. Then he broke it and gave it to them. Suddenly, their eyes were opened, and they recognized him. And at that moment he disappeared! They said to each other, "Didn't our hearts burn within us as he talked with us on the road and explained the Scriptures to us?" And within the*

*hour they were on their way back to Jerusalem. There they found the eleven disciples and the others who had gathered with them, who said, "The Lord has really risen! He appeared to Peter." Then the two from Emmaus told their story of how Jesus had appeared to them as they were walking along the road, and how they had recognized him as he was breaking the bread.*

As the two men excitedly told the disciples how Jesus had appeared to them, Jesus suddenly appeared again:

## LUKE 24:36-53 (NLT)

*And just as they were telling about it, Jesus himself was suddenly standing there among them. "Peace be with you," he said. But the whole group was startled and frightened, thinking they were seeing a ghost! "Why are you frightened?" he asked. "Why are your hearts filled with doubt? Look at my hands. Look at my feet. You can see that it's really me. Touch me and make sure that I am not a ghost, because*

*ghosts don't have bodies, as you see that I do."*
*As he spoke, he showed them his hands and*
*his feet. Still they stood there in disbelief, filled*
*with joy and wonder. Then he asked them, "Do*
*you have anything here to eat?" They gave him*
*a piece of broiled fish, and he ate it as they*
*watched. Then he said, "When I was with you*
*before, I told you that everything written about*
*me in the law of Moses and the prophets and in*
*the Psalms must be fulfilled." Then he opened*
*their minds to understand the Scriptures. And*
*he said, "Yes, it was written long ago that the*
*Messiah would suffer and die and rise from the*
*dead on the third day. It was also written that*
*this message would be proclaimed in the author-*
*ity of his name to all the nations, beginning*
*in Jerusalem: 'There is forgiveness of sins for*
*all who repent.' You are witnesses of all these*
*things. And now I will send the Holy Spirit,*
*just as my Father promised. But stay here in the*
*city until the Holy Spirit comes and fills you*
*with power from heaven." Then Jesus led them*
*to Bethany, and lifting his hands to heaven, he*
*blessed them. While he was blessing them, he*

*left them and was taken up to heaven. So they worshiped him and then returned to Jerusalem filled with great joy. And they spent all of their time in the Temple, praising God.*

Jesus walked and talked with people and many completely recognized Him. He ate food. And boom. He walked right through a wall. Don't you love it? Jesus walked *right through a wall.* There's nothing normal about that! The disciples freaked out. After the shock of seeing Him go through a wall, they thought Jesus was a spirit. To prove otherwise, Jesus said, "Feel me. A spirit doesn't have flesh and bone." Where was His blood? He left it at the mercy seat for you and me.

"How do you know Jesus walked through a wall?" somebody asks. Verse 36 says as the two followers of Jesus were telling the disciples what happened on the road to Emmaus, Jesus was "suddenly standing there among them" and greeted them. He sure didn't knock on the door! He didn't need to knock.

Did you also notice the first thing on Jesus' mind? After explaining He wasn't a ghost, His first question was, "Got anything to eat?" He wanted to know where the meat was. He didn't ask about kale or salad. No, Jesus was asking, "Where's the beef?"

Sometimes Christians have this tendency to think that when we are raptured, we will all go to heaven and become like robots, losing all personality. No. Some people think we will lounge around on fluffy clouds playing harps all cherub-like. No. Religious tradition has given us some crazy, totally unscriptural ideas. (Check out *End Times Made Easy* where we share how supernaturally natural the Millennium will be.)

Listen to me now. Jesus was showing the disciples—and you—just how supernaturally natural the glorified body is. Jesus was showing you His glorified body as a picture of your future. He was showing you that you won't be a ghost. You will still have an appetite. You will walk right through walls. You will still have muscle and bone and will still be recognized. How cool is that?

> Jesus was showing the disciples—and you—just how supernaturally natural the glorified body is.

As I travel teaching on end times, there's one question I get more than any other. A sweet little lady will almost always raise her hand and ask, "Will I know my husband in heaven?"

I usually answer, "Do you want to know your husband in heaven?"

The real answer is of course you will. You will carry everything from here to there. You will get a new body, but you won't forget everything you know. You will not turn into a freak. Listen, if you like sports, you will play sports. If you like music, you can learn all the instruments. If you like art, you will paint masterpieces. Life with Jesus will be more glorious than you can possibly imagine.

I tell you right now that for the first six months of the Millennium, I'm going to play at St. Andrews Golf Club. I will be translated to Augusta, Georgia, to the National Golf Club there, then I'll be going on to Hawaii, and translated back to St. Andrews. I can play all these courses back to back because it won't get dark. I can golf 24 hours a day.

"Will you really want to do that?" somebody asks. Yes! You see, when it comes to heaven and the

Millennium, some people's thinking is so weird and distorted. Many people do not understand that God wants you to enjoy yourself. Just as it thrills me to see my daughter happy, it thrills God to see His children happy, joyful, smiling, laughing, and enjoying life.

When you understand that about Him, it's easier to understand how awesome the Millennium will be. Man, you will experience some fulfillment. A while back I played the guitar, and although I wasn't very good, I really had fun playing old rock songs from the '70s. I had some different guitars over the years, but at one point, I had a Fender Strat until the Lord said, "Give it away." He said, "Give it to that guy right there." As it turned out, the young man had just asked his mom for a guitar that day, and his mom said, "Well, believe God for it!"

Over the years, I would buy a guitar, give away a guitar, and buy a cooler one. As I walked into the music store one day thinking I would buy another guitar, the Lord said to me, "Why don't you learn to play every instrument? You're going to live forever." I was like, *Whoa*. It kind of messed with me.

Think about that. God is giving you a glorified body to get your flesh ready for forever.

Remember the cherubim and the seraphim around the throne of God that I mentioned earlier? The seraphim covered the mercy seat—two wings that cover the face, two wings that cover the feet, and two wings that fly. They cry, "Holy, holy, holy." How would you like to have a job like that 24/7? Right now, your flesh, the rods and cones in your eyes, and so much more cannot handle the brightness or the magnificent presence of God. So how wonderful that God will make you a brand-new body retrofitted to handle the glory of God.

Throughout the Scriptures, we read that when people encountered God, they hit the floor or the ground. Daniel had to be picked up a couple of times. Ezekiel had to be picked up—once by his hair. Their human bodies could not handle the glory of God, so God will retrofit our bodies to handle His presence. A retrofitted body is a matter of functionality to go before the throne of God.

Imagine this. The Bible says there is no need for the sun in heaven because of the glory that's in His face (Rev. 21:23). Wow. I believe in heaven we will think, *The sun is coming up! No, no. It's Jesus walking toward us.* In Him it pleased the Father that all the fullness of the Godhead would dwell bodily (Col. 1:19). Whoooo! Hallelujah!

Travel will be a whole different experience as well. Like angels, we will be able to instantly be somewhere else. Remember angels do always behold the face of their Father for the children they protect (Matt. 18:10). So, obviously, angels travel back and forth from heaven to earth pretty quickly, and we will too.

The Word of God doesn't give us every detail about our futures, but we already read where Jesus' glorified body walks through walls, eats, and behaves normally. In John 21:5, Jesus yelled from the shore, asking, "Have you caught any fish?" He didn't make weird, eerie noises like we would expect in some scary Hollywood movie: "Ooooooh, woooo" all muffled and ghostlike. No. Peter recognized Him instantly and yelled, "It's Jesus!" as he jumped out of the boat and swam over to Him (John 21:7).

> **The Word of God doesn't give us every detail about our futures, but we already read where Jesus' glorified body walks through walls, eats, and behaves normally.**

Peter did not yell, "Aaaah, it's a freak!" Too often we let our minds take the freaky route rather than the normal route. Anything God plans for us will be very, very cool! God loves to put a little stamp right on our beautiful hope that we will be with Him forever.

# FEAST CALENDAR POINTS TO RAPTURE TIMING

To bless and strengthen our hope for Jesus' return, let's consider the calendar of feasts, which shows us something important about the timing of the Rapture. Why are the feasts indicative of Rapture timing? First, Jesus has flawlessly fulfilled every single feast. Second, feasts are dress rehearsals. Most weddings and plays have dress rehearsals, so everyone knows their positions, cues, and lines. God also gives us rehearsals for what's ahead.

The first Bible feast is the **Passover,** a major event even today on the Jewish calendar. It was instituted by God to commemorate the deliverance of the Israelites from Egyptian bondage and saving of the firstborn from the destroyer (Exodus 12, 13, 23, 34). A lamb without blemish was killed—both as a sacrifice and a symbol of Jesus the Lamb of God at Calvary on Passover. As the blood was applied to Israeli doorposts, the death angel literally *passed over* those homes. Jesus is the Lamb of God who took away the sin of the world and was sacrificed for us on Passover.

The next feast was the **Feast of Unleavened Bread.** The Israelites took three pieces of bread and folded the middle piece, pierced it, and broke it. This is symbolic of Jesus the Bread of Life born in Bethlehem. *Bethlehem* means home of the bread. Isn't it cool? The **Feast of the First Fruits** followed to celebrate the first fruits of harvest.

Normally, a crucifixion takes longer than when Jesus was on the cross. Criminals were hung on the cross and a slow death was part of the spectacle—a sort of crime deterrent. But Jesus had a feast to keep! Jesus hung on the cross, taking our sin, poverty, and sickness upon Himself and then died quickly on **Passover.** He was buried at the **Feast of Unleavened Bread**, and He rose again on the **Feast of First Fruits**.

Jesus met the timing of each feast flawlessly, which had been prophesied. When you talk to a Jewish person about this, it freaks them out because it proves Jesus is the Messiah.

The next feast is **Pentecost** where the Holy Ghost was poured out. Is there another feast that has not yet been fulfilled? Yes, the **Feast of Trumpets or Rosh Hashanah or Feast of Gatherings**. The word *Rosh Hashanah* in Hebrew literally means "head of the year." The biblical name is *Yom Teruah* or literally "day of shouting or blasting." I believe the Rapture of the Church will take place on the **Feast of Trumpets.**

Somebody might say, "If you know that, then you would know when the Rapture will be." Yes, that is exactly right. I know exactly when the Feast of Trumpets starts in Israel and when it's finished, and the whole time each year I'm on high alert. I've said to the Lord, "Hmm, this is a perfect time for You to come." There are several things about Feast of Trumpets that make sense for the Rapture to occur during that time.

Of course, I don't know the specific year the Lord is coming back. I would never preach that! That's crazy! But I can tell you with great confidence that whatever year Jesus chooses to return, it will probably be during the Feast of Trumpets. If I am wrong, you can correct me as we are on our way up in the air. We can sit down and talk it over in heaven.

> But I can tell you with great confidence that whatever year Jesus chooses to return, it will probably be during the Feast of Trumpets.

Let me explain why I think this way. Number one, the Feast of Trumpets represents the beginning of a coronation of a king. In any coronation, there is always a private ceremony for the family and a public ceremony for everyone else. When we are raptured, we will attend a private ceremony where Jesus will be coronated King of Kings and Lord of Lords. At the Second Coming, Jesus will be presented to the whole earth in a public ceremony as the King of Kings and the Lord of Lords.

The next event is the start of **Seven Days of Awe** before the **Day of Atonement**. That's a picture of the seven years of Tribulation. In other words, the Church is raptured, and there are seven days of awe for the rest of the world. That's a perfect correlation to seven years of Tribulation.

The Feast of Trumpets always falls 29.5 days after the last new moon, but they never knew exactly which day it would be. They didn't know whether it would fall on the 29th or the 30th of the month because it was so many days from the previous one. The Sanhedrin, a tribunal assembly in every ancient city of Israel with religious, civil, and criminal jurisdiction, would go out with two witnesses to determine when the new moon was and announce it. That's why Jesus said no one knows the day or the hour. He was talking about the Feast of Trumpets.

The Sanhedrin would go outside, look up in the sky together, and then complain, "Not yet! It's not today!" Then one day, they would look in the sky and say, "This is it! It's today!" So when Jesus said, "*No one knows the day or hour when these things will happen, not even the angels in heaven or the Son himself*" (Matt. 24:36 NLT), they all knew that Jesus was referring to the Feast of Trumpets. Jesus was trying to give the Church a clue that you will be raptured on the Feast of Trumpets.

Once again someone might say, "Well, if you know that, then you know when the Lord is coming back." Yes, that's right! Just like you knew when your wedding was, you know when the Groom is coming for His Bride, the Church, and you know when you will be raptured. I know that freaks people out, but it's true just the same.

Recently, I made that statement and a lady blinked at me like a frog in a west Texas hailstorm, as Brother Hagin used to say. People are so shocked on all these topics because the Church either has not been taught or has been taught incorrectly about Jesus' return and the timing of it all.

The next feast is the **Feast of Tabernacles,** which in Jewish history recognized God's salvation, shelter, provision, and faithfulness. I believe the Second Coming will happen during the timing of the Feast of Tabernacles when Jesus returns and bodily tabernacles with men.

But listen to me! The Rapture is signless, but for the Second Coming, there is sign after sign after sign. It is so wonderful that we have all these things coming to pass in our lifetime. Think about it. You never have to die.

# BIBLE PRECEDENT OF RAPTURES

The Christian world has come up with so many weird doctrines about the Rapture because it is unusual. Then again, just because it's unusual does not mean it is unscriptural. Enoch was raptured. Elijah was raptured. And the Church will be raptured. In fact, let's look at some Bible examples of rapture.

Elisha and the sons of the prophets knew the very day Elijah would be raptured. Second Kings 2:1 says, "*When the Lord was about to take Elijah up to heaven in a whirlwind, Elijah and Elisha were traveling from Gilgal*" (NLT).

Notice this conversation between Elijah and Elisha in 2 Kings 2:9–12 (NLT):

*When they came to the other side, Elijah said to Elisha, "Tell me what I can do for you before I am taken away." And Elisha replied, "Please let me inherit a double share of your spirit and become your successor." "You have asked a difficult thing," Elijah replied. "If you see me when I am taken from you, then you will get your request. But if not, then you won't." As they were walking along and talking, suddenly a chariot of fire appeared, drawn by horses of fire. It drove between the two men, separating them, and Elijah was carried by a whirlwind into heaven. Elisha saw it and cried out, "My father! My father! I see the chariots and chari-oteers of Israel!" And as they disappeared from sight, Elisha tore his clothes in distress.*

The Bible says Enoch walked by faith and was a spokesman for God, making him a perfect type or symbol of the Church. He also had a son named Methuselah, but Enoch departed right before the flood came. Genesis 5:24 says, "And Enoch walked with God: and *he was not;* for God took him." Notice what Hebrews says below.

## HEBREWS 11:5 (NLT)

*It was by faith that Enoch was taken up to heaven without dying—"he disappeared, because God took him." For before he was taken up, he was known as a person who pleased God.*

How would you like to have job prophesying about the Second Coming of the Lord before Jesus even came the first time? Talk about awkward! Imagine telling people that Jesus will come back with 10,000 saints while people are asking, "Who's coming back? What saints? We don't know any saints." Enoch had to preach like that, and then he was taken to heaven without dying, caught up because the wickedness of the day was so bad that God took him off the earth.

## GENESIS 5:22-24 (NLT)

*After the birth of Methuselah, Enoch lived in close fellowship with God for another 300 years, and he had other sons and daughters. Enoch lived 365 years, walking in close fellowship with God. Then one day he disappeared, because God took him.*

Enoch was taken off the earth. Elijah was taken off the earth. These two aren't the only raptures in the Bible. The New Testament tells how Jesus and His disciples sang together—"When they had sung a hymn, they went out to the Mount of Olives" (Matt. 26:30 NKJV), where Jesus left for heaven. Jesus Himself was raptured.

## ACTS 1:1-3 (NLT) SAYS:

*In my first book I told you, Theophilus, about everything Jesus began to do and teach until the day he was taken up to heaven after giving his chosen apostles further instructions through the Holy Spirit. During the forty days after he suffered and died, he appeared to the apostles from* time to time, and he proved to them in many ways that he was actually alive. And he talked to them about the Kingdom of God.

Then Acts 1:8-11 (NLT) says:

*"But you will receive power when the Holy Spirit comes upon you. And you will be my witnesses, telling people about me everywhere—in Jerusalem, throughout Judea, in Samaria, and to the ends of the earth." After saying this, he was taken up into a cloud while they were watching, and they could no longer see him. As they strained to see him rising into heaven, two white-robed men suddenly stood among them. "Men of Galilee," they said, "why are you standing here staring into heaven? Jesus has been taken from you into heaven, but someday he will return from heaven in the same way you saw him go!"*

Jesus compared the Second Coming to the days of Lot and the days of Noah. Notice what the angel told Lot.

## GENESIS 19:15-24 (NLT)

*At dawn the next morning the angels became insistent. "Hurry," they said to Lot. "Take your wife and your two daughters who are here. Get out right now, or you will be swept away in the destruction of the city!" When Lot still hesitated, the angels seized his hand and the hands of his wife and two daughters and rushed them to safety outside the city, for the Lord was merciful. When they were safely out of the city, one of the angels ordered, "Run for your lives! And don't look back or stop anywhere in the valley! Escape to the mountains, or you will be swept away!" "Oh no, my lord!" Lot begged. "You have been so gracious to me and saved my life, and you have shown such great kindness. But I cannot go to the mountains. Disaster would catch up to me there, and I would soon die. See, there is a small village nearby. Please let me go there instead; don't you see how small it is? Then my life will be saved." "All right," the angel said, "I will grant your request. I will not destroy the little village. But hurry! Escape to it, for I can do nothing until you arrive there."*

*(This explains why that village was known as Zoar, which means "little place.") Lot reached the village just as the sun was rising over the horizon. Then the Lord rained down fire and burning sulfur from the sky on Sodom and Gomorrah.*

The angel told Lot that he *could not* do anything until the righteous departed, and Noah rode the flood of sin, corruption, and torrential rains like the righteous who endure. Both are perfect pictures of the Church leaving and Israel riding through the Tribulation period for seven years. God is so cool to give us clues!

The Bible talks about more raptures during the Tribulation. The two witnesses will be caught up to heaven (Rev. 11) so there is ample biblical precedent that people on earth, all of a sudden, leave earth and depart to heaven.

The Greek word for *rapture* is actually *harpazo*,[1] which means "snatched up or caught up." Interestingly enough, however, the word *rapture* is not in the literal Greek, but in the Latin the word *rapture* means "to be caught up or snatched." Think about it—walking with God and then shooo! Think of all the *Invasion of the Body Snatchers*-type movies. I'm sure folks will come up with a bunch of New Age explanations for why people have disappeared after the Rapture. But no matter what you call it, how wonderful that God will evacuate you because of what's getting ready to happen on the earth.

> I'm sure folks will come up with a bunch of New Age explanations for why people have disappeared after the Rapture.

## 1 THESSALONIANS 5:9-11

*For God hath not appointed us to wrath, but to obtain salvation by our Lord Jesus Christ, who died for us, that, whether we wake or sleep, we should live together with him. Wherefore comfort yourselves together, and edify one another, even as also ye do.*

Verse 11 drives home the point once again that we are to comfort and edify fellow Christians with this news. The teaching of the Rapture was always to bring comfort—never fear. Yet today, there is a religious mentality that has crept into the Church where so many people are afraid of the coming of the Lord. People often come up to me in meetings and say, "I was afraid to come. I thought it was going to be bad news." But, again, there is no bad news for the Christian!

# WALLS OF HUMANITY CHANGE

I think the Rapture scene will look something like when the devil disputed with the angel for the body of Moses (Jude 9). After the devil argued over Moses' body, the archangel said, "The Lord rebuke you." I believe Lucifer will say, "Hey, these Christians are here on the earth, and I have charge over this earth." But the archangel will say, "The Lord rebuke you!" I believe that's what was meant in 1 Thessalonians 4:16 when it said "with the voice of an archangel." All of a sudden, the walls of humanity will change.

There's a picture of this in the Old Covenant when Israel walked around the walls of Jericho shouting until the walls came down. In the same way, we will step into an eternal-type body—never to be troubled with the scar of the fall again. Talk about shouting! We should shout right now! In a moment of time, all the horribleness of this dispensation will disappear from us. No more death. No more sickness. No more separation. Our veins will no longer be filled with blood—the glory of God will course through them. Life will no longer be in the blood but in God's glory! How glorious is that?

> In a moment of time, all the horribleness of this dispensation will disappear from us. No more death. No more sickness. No more separation.

# THE CHURCH IS A RESTRAINING FORCE

Paul shares more detailed information and revelation with us in 2 Thessalonians 2:1-3:

> *Now we beseech you, brethren, by **the coming of our Lord** [the Second Coming] Jesus Christ, and by **our gathering together unto him**, [the Rapture of the Church because we will be gathered together unto Him] that ye be not soon shaken in mind, or be troubled, neither by spirit, nor by word, nor by letter as from us, as that the day of Christ is at hand. Let no man deceive you by any means: for that day shall not come, except there come **a falling away** first, and that man of sin be revealed, the son of perdition.*

Notice again that this passage tells us of two events: "the coming of the Lord" refers to the Second Coming and "our gathering unto Him" refers to the Rapture. Let me also call your attention to the phrase "a falling away" in verse 3. The Greek word there is *apostasia* or "the apostasy." Is there a difference between *apostasy* and *the apostasy* or *apostasia*? Yes! *Apostasy* is a departing from the faith. *Apostasia* is the exact word used when Enoch departed before the flood, and it means departing, period—as in an exit—goodbye.

This verse did not refer to departing from the flood. If a departing from the faith could have brought the Antichrist, he would have come during the Dark Ages. The apostle Paul is saying here that the Antichrist cannot even be revealed until the Church departs. The moment the Church does depart, Satan is in power and has full access to everything. The Church is a restraining force in the earth, and the devil for this time is being held in check by the Church.

Christian friend, you have so much authority that God must pull you off the earth before the seven-year Tribulation or you would be dictating what happens on the earth. You would be redirecting asteroids.

"Where in the world do you come up with that?" somebody asks. In James 5, Elijah prayed

Christian friend, you have so much authority that God must pull you off the earth before the seven-year Tribulation or you would be dictating what happens on the earth. You would be redirecting asteroids.

that it would not rain for three and a half years, and it didn't rain for three and a half years. That's a picture of the Church. If Elijah can dictate natural rain, we can dictate spiritual rain. That whole chapter is about the dominion we have as the body of Christ on the earth.

God must take the Church off the earth so the Antichrist can come on the scene because He gives the devil the last part—or three and a half years—of the Tribulation. Jesus had three and a half years, and the Antichrist will have three and a half years. The Antichrist will function the three and a half years on his own or with demonic influence, but then Lucifer will go bodily into the Antichrist and incarnate him. Just like Jesus took on flesh, Lucifer will take on flesh. Again, that cannot happen while the Church is on earth because we have so much power.

Let's read a little further in 2 Thessalonians 2:7-8 (NLT):

*For this lawlessness is already at work secretly, and it will remain secret until the one who is holding it back steps out of the way. Then the man of lawlessness will be revealed, but the Lord Jesus will slay him with the breath of his mouth and destroy him by the splendor of his coming.*

Man, I love what is ahead for Lucifer. His future is pretty bleak, and he deserves every bit of it. He was defeated 2,000 years ago, but he's going to get the absolute tar beat out of him at the Second Coming. He will be thrown in that pit, and I, for one, will be throwing garbage down in the pit. I'm going to become a garbage man in the Millennium. "What do you do, Brother Joe?" "I grab up all the garbage I can find to throw at Lucifer."

The thought pattern in God's Word is straight-forward about the Rapture: The Church has an appointment. We are expected at the Reward Seat of Jesus Christ. I've heard people say, "Yes, but the Church must be here for the Tribulation period because it is to purify us." No true! The Tribulation period is to motivate the Jews to accept the Messiah. As a Christian, I've already accepted Jesus as my Messiah; I don't need to go through the pressure. Clearly, the purpose of the seven-year Tribulation is pressure because some people are so hardheaded, they won't change unless they are relentlessly clobbered or pelted.

During World War II, this type of thinking was called a foxhole mentality. Soldiers might wonder if there is a God or choose not to serve Him until the gun battles ramped up. When soldiers were crouched in a foxhole with missiles flying straight at them, most soldiers changed their minds and thought, *Well, this is a good time to get saved—like NOW!*

Yeah right, it's a good time to get saved because you think you're about to die. During the Tribulation, there will be seven years of that kind of pressure and a whole lot more. But you see, you and I don't need to be here for that because we've already accepted Jesus as Lord and Savior.

## RAPTURED IN THE FALL

I honestly believe that come fall of whatever year, there will be such a joy and an unction in the Church that Jesus is about to come. There will be such an anticipation in the Church, and we will be sensing, *Wow! This is it! We are about to meet Him face to face!* For those of us who are married, we can think about how we acted right before our wedding. It will be the same for all of us as the Bride of Christ.

Before a wedding, the bride and groom usually go through a couple of days of reflection before they say "I do." I believe it will be the same for the Christian who says, "Wow. Big change is coming!" All of a sudden, we will be caught up in the air to attend the Reward Seat of Christ, and Jesus will be crowned King of Kings right before us.

We will stand in front of Jesus face to face. We will see the scars on His hands and the crown on

His head, and we'll think, *How could it be that He chose to die for me?* We will worship Him like we've never worshipped before, and there will be honor and dominion and power unto the Son of God who was and is and is to come. The fulfillment of our redemption will take place right then and there.

Listen to me now! The Rapture will be a beginning—not an ending. You are not done when you are raptured, which is why you have so much in your heart yet to do. Somebody says, "I don't want the Rapture to happen yet. I have so many things I still want to do for Jesus." You feel that way because you are not done. (I share more on this topic in my book *End Times Made Easy*.) Friend, you are just beginning to taste the powers of the world to come.

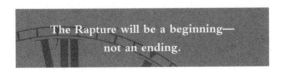

The Rapture will be a beginning—not an ending.

What happens when you get just one bite of your favorite big, juicy cheeseburger or favorite sandwich? You want more! You get just a taste, and you get irritable doing without. "I want the whole cheeseburger," you say. That's where you are right now in time. You've had a bite of what's to come spiritually, and you want more. Right now, you are in the process of learning the ways of God because you've got such a great big change coming.

You, Christian friend, you are about to be raptured.

# CHAPTER 3

# THE SECOND COMING OF JESUS

The first time Jesus came to earth, His entrance was as low-key as possible. There was no place for Him at the inn, and the King of Kings was born in a manger—a livestock shack surrounded by hay and animals. King Jesus laid aside all His heavenly privileges and power to humbly take on flesh to rescue you and me. Jesus was not recognized as the Messiah by His own people during His earthly ministry. Instead, He was mocked, beaten, and crucified. But the Second Coming will be a whole different story. This time, Jesus will be welcomed with the pomp and circumstance deserving of a king. Let's put it this way: The Boss is coming back to the planet, and His return will be spectacular—the grand-finale event of the universe.

> The Boss is coming back to the planet, and His return will be spectacular—the grand-finale event of the universe.

We don't really know the protocol for receiving a heavenly King who comes to earth. How does nature even receive the One who created nature? For thousands of years, man has built edifices to honor himself, but how will we honor Jesus when He returns? Every knee will bow in adoration and every tongue will confess that Jesus Christ is Lord to the glory of God the Father.

Every book in the Bible foretells that Jesus is coming again. Hosea gave you a picture. Malachi gave you a picture. Zephaniah gave you a picture. Joel gave you a picture. All the prophets pointed to the Second Coming, and it's so cool how God gave you different glimpses of just how grand it will be. What a great privilege that we will return with Jesus at the Second Coming—alongside Him on white horses to help the King implement His kingdom.

John described Jesus' return this way, and it's hard to imagine anything cooler.

## REVELATION 19:11-16 (MSG)

*Then I saw Heaven open wide—and oh! a white horse and its Rider. The Rider, named Faithful and True, judges and makes war in pure righteousness. His eyes are a blaze of fire, on his head many crowns. He has a Name inscribed that's known only to himself. He is dressed in a robe soaked with blood, and he is addressed as "Word of God." The armies of Heaven, mounted on white horses and dressed in dazzling white linen, follow him. A sharp sword comes out of his mouth so he can subdue the nations, then rule them with a rod of iron. He treads the winepress of the raging wrath of God, the Sovereign-Strong. On his robe and thigh is written, King of kings, Lord of lords.*

Did you see yourself? You're in verse 14 where it said the "armies of heaven." You will follow Jesus, "mounted on white horses and dressed in dazzling white linen." Maybe you've never ridden a horse before in this life, but you will be riding the coolest horse you've ever seen in the next one.

When I was a kid, my family had an appaloosa that was demon-possessed. I'm kidding, but everybody who got on him got bucked off. I had to climb a tree to get on that horse. I climbed out over the limbs, and the second I got on him, pshooo, he shot me back off. But the horses in heaven somehow yield to instruction, and we're going to fly on those horses right along with Jesus. Wow.

The brightness of His glory will be so magnificent that there will be no need for the sun. The glory will radiate from Jesus' face. Jesus will be wearing crowns on His head and white robes. Talk about pomp and circumstance.

You and I and the Church of Jesus Christ will be right there behind Him, coming from heaven down to earth. There will be no shadows anywhere

You and I and the Church of Jesus Christ will be right there behind Him, coming from heaven down to earth.

because He Himself permeates light everywhere as He leads the charge back to earth.

The universe has been expanding at the speed of light for some 13 to 16 billion years. Between Genesis 1 and Genesis 2, there was no time. As far as the universe has spun out, we know there are about 100 billion galaxies with 100 billion stars like our sun, but God calls them all by name. The universe and the heavens will bow. All creation is waiting for the Creator to come. And, all of a sudden, He comes.

All creation and the hearts of men will bow in adoration. The saints will come marching in. After the Rapture, you will have attended the Reward Seat of Christ and be retrofitted for your future when Jesus reigns for a thousand years. You will have attended the Marriage Supper of the Lamb, the greatest party you've ever been to in your entire life.

Then, suddenly, orders will come from headquarters. The regiment of your city and state will be told to rise up on horses, and the excitement will build with every person, saying, "Wow! It's time! We're going back to the earth with God! It's time! It's time! We're returning with our King of Kings and Lord of Lords."

In a flash, we will descend out of heaven on horses and come reeling down through the universe. We'll see this little spot down there called planet Earth, where the Antichrist is looking stupid and doing evil everywhere evil can be done. As he looks up, he will see Someone brighter than all the 100 billion stars coming right straight at him. It will look like the light on a freight train, and behind that freight train are you and me traveling with *Jesus.*

The Antichrist will think he still can defeat Jesus but is he in for an epic surprise. You can imagine the Antichrist's staff saying, "What is that coming at us? Is it a missile? No, it's white and blindingly bright. Are those horses?" Talk about a missile—it will be dressed in light hurling toward the planet. My friend, you will be rockin' right from heaven down to earth, and what a view you will have.

The earth will make preparation for that grand entrance of God Himself. The mountains will be leveled. There will be no more islands. There will be great earthquakes. The earth will go through a cataclysmic earthquake and shake like crazy. Jesus will stand at the Mount of Olives and a great earthquake will split apart the mountain with a great valley between the two. King Jesus will stand there with a scepter of righteousness as the scepter of His kingdom, and He will set up His kingdom right then and there. Instantly, He will bring peace into the earth and stop war. Right there, it's eradicated. Wow!

> King Jesus will stand there with a scepter of righteousness as the scepter of His kingdom, and He will set up His kingdom right then and there.

Lucifer will say, "I think I messed this deal up." How true—even though it's probably the only truth he's ever told. Can't you hear Lucifer saying, "I'm bailing on this deal. I lose every time. I have been stupid," before Jesus obliterates him with the brightness of His coming. Hallelujah! Amen! Glory to our King of Kings!

It will be the coolest thing ever, and you will be an eyewitness!

Every movie you've ever seen where the hero flies in at the end to save the day comes from right here. Jesus will return and stop a war. There will be no more war because Jesus is the Prince of Peace.

Wow.

What a great privilege we will have to return with Jesus to help the King implement His kingdom. How cool that you will be raised up to be an overseers of His wonderful kingdom for a thousand years. There are great things ahead for all of us. It's an amazing time in history that you and I were chosen to live—right before God physically comes back to the planet.

# GRANDDADDY OF ALL EVENTS

There's no question that the Second Coming will be dramatic. Matthew described it this way.

# MATTHEW 24:27 (NLT)

*For as the lightning flashes in the east and shines to the west, so it will be when the Son of Man comes.*

Have you ever seen lightning that was casual? There's no such thing as a casual lightning bolt. While preaching in Virginia a while back, I stood in front of a window in the place where I stayed. This bolt of lightning hit a tree about 20 feet away, and the hair on the back of my head stood straight up. *Kaboom.* Electricity shot out, and the power went out in the entire vicinity. There was nothing casual about it; it got my attention. I didn't go, "Hmmm. What was that?" I knew exactly what it was that almost fried me.

The Second Coming will be the granddaddy of events throughout the universe—throughout all eternity. Skip down a few verses.

The Second Coming will be the granddaddy of events throughout the universe—throughout all eternity.

# MATTHEW 24:29-31 (NLT):

*Immediately after the anguish of those days, the sun will be darkened, the moon will give no light, the stars will fall from the sky, and the powers in the heavens will be shaken. And then at last, the sign that the Son of Man is coming will appear in the heavens, and there will be deep mourning among all the peoples of the earth. And they will see the Son of Man coming on the clouds of heaven with power and great glory. And he will send out his angels with the mighty blast of a trumpet, and they will gather his chosen ones from all over the world—from the farthest ends of the earth and heaven.*

The Message quotes verses 29-31 this way:

*Following those hard times, sun will fade out, moon cloud over, stars fall out of the sky, cosmic powers tremble. Then, the Arrival of the Son of Man! It will fill the skies—no one will miss it. Unready people all over the world, outsiders to the splendor and power, will raise a huge lament as they watch the*

*Son of Man blazing out of heaven. At that same moment, he'll dispatch his angels with a trumpet-blast summons, pulling in God's chosen from the four winds, from pole to pole.*

The Second Coming will be the complete opposite of the Rapture. At the Rapture of the Church, the righteous are taken off the earth and into heaven. At the Second Coming, the wicked are plucked off the earth so Jesus can begin His kingdom on earth with all righteous people.

Remember what He said, "I let the wheat grow with the tares and, at the end of the age, I'll let the angels be the reapers" (Matt. 13:24-30). All of a sudden here, Jesus will set up the angels to be the reapers at the end of the Tribulation period. People who have not repented despite all the signs and warnings will be separated as the wheat from the chaff.

The righteous, natural-bodied people who make it through the latter part of the Tribulation will enter the kingdom of God on the earth. The arrival of these people into the kingdom is a huge deal for you and me because they will be the new kids on the block for a thousand years, and we will be implementing the kingdom and preaching to them. When they reach the age of accountability, they will still have the nature of Adam in them and need to be born again.

You'll be able to say to them, "There's Jesus right there. Get saved!" Christians are sometimes tempted to think our work will be finished at the Rapture, but we have a whole 1,000 years beyond. If you're tasting of the powers of the world to come, you will be operating in much more in the world to come. Going to heaven is not the end of it all—really, it's just the beginning.

> Going to heaven is not the end of it all—really, it's just the beginning.

# ISAIAH'S RENDITION OF THE SECOND COMING

We will return to Matthew 24 shortly, but let's go to Isaiah and look at some Old Testament verses

that are very graphic and exact. This is Isaiah's ren-
dition of what the Second Coming will look like.

## ISAIAH 2:1-4 (NLT)

*This is a vision that Isaiah son of Amoz saw
concerning Judah and Jerusalem: In the last
days, the mountain of the Lord's house will be
the highest of all—the most important place on
earth. It will be raised above the other hills, and
people from all over the world will stream there
to worship. People from many nations will come
and say, "Come, let us go up to the mountain of
the Lord, to the house of Jacob's God. There he
will teach us his ways, and we will walk in his
paths." For the Lord's teaching will go out from
Zion; his word will go out from Jerusalem. The
Lord will mediate between nations and will
settle international disputes. They will hammer
their swords into plowshares and their spears
into pruning hooks. Nation will no longer fight
against nation, nor train for war anymore.*

Notice the picture of the new earth that Isaiah is creating for us. That's why he wrote this and

prophesied this for us. When the Prince of Peace returns, everything is altered. People are deciding, "Let's go up to Jerusalem and worship. This is the event of all events to see the King of Kings and Lord of Lords."

# SEVEN STAGES OF THE SECOND COMING

When discussing the Second Coming of the Lord, many people think Jesus will return to the Mount of Olives and that's it, but in reality, there are several stages of the Second Coming.

- **Stage 1:** During the latter part of the Tribulation, allies of the Antichrist assemble for the Battle of Armageddon. Jesus comes back to stop them!

- **Stage 2:** Commercial Babylon is destroyed. There are four or five protocols right here before Jesus sets foot on the earth.

- **Stage 3:** Jerusalem falls and is ravaged.

- **Stage 4:** The Antichrist moves south to attack

the remnant because during that time Israel goes down into Bosra to receive protection.

- **Stage 5:** In glory, Jesus returns to the Mount of Olives where He was crucified.

- **Stage 6:** Jesus obliterates Lucifer with the brightness of His coming.

- **Stage 7:** Jesus instigates cleansing of the Temple.

Look with me at Zechariah 13 and 14 to read about these stages of the Second Coming in more detail. It's not good news at all, but it's good to know. Actually, Zechariah 14 is one of the most graphic depictions of the Second Coming in all the Bible, but Zechariah 13 sets the stage for it.

We read about stage three in Zechariah 13:7-8:

*Awake, O sword, against my shepherd, and against the man that is my fellow, saith the Lord of hosts: smite the shepherd, and the sheep shall be scattered: and I will turn mine hand upon the little ones. And it shall come to pass, that in all the land, saith the Lord,*

*two parts therein shall be cut off and die; but*
*the third shall be left therein.*

Zechariah is prophesying that right before the Second Coming, two thirds of all of Israel will get killed. In other words, there's another holocaust coming. We don't preach about that very much, but only a third of them will remain through the latter part of the Tribulation. This is sobering!

There are approximately six million Jews living in Israel now. If four million are killed, then two million would remain. Keep in mind that we are seeing the different phases of the Second Coming here and different events are happening in each stage. The Antichrist will be dealt with, Babylon will be dealt with, and Jerusalem will be ravaged. There are actually five or six depictions of that, and it literally says four million Jews will be killed.

In stage four, the Antichrist moves south to attack the remnant because during that time Israel goes down into Bosra to receive protection. When the Antichrist goes down there, stage five takes place, which is pretty radical. Jesus returns in glory to the Mount of Olives, the very mountain where He was crucified. How cool is that? The seventh and final phase that we know is the Battle of Armageddon.

We read earlier in Matthew 24 about Jesus returning at the end of the Battle of Armageddon. The Antichrist thinks he can win, but all of a sudden, Jesus comes back as lightning from heaven. Lucifer is so stupid that he still thinks he can beat Jesus but quickly learns otherwise.

During these different stages of the Second Coming, Jesus rescues the remnant. I really like one of the depictions in Tim LaHaye's *Left Behind* series. It's as cool as it gets. I know it's fiction, but it brings to life Jesus slaying the enemy with the sword of His mouth (Rev. 19:15).

In the *Left Behind* movie, Jesus walks through the valley of Armageddon saying, "I am the root of Jesse. I am He who was and is and is to come." Come on! Jesus begins quoting Himself: "I am Stephen's signs and wonders. I am Peter's shadow. In Genesis, I was the seed of a woman. In Exodus, I was the Passover Lamb. In Leviticus, I was the High Priest. In Numbers, I was the pillar of cloud by day and the pillar of fire by night."

In the depiction, as Jesus is quoting Himself, armies start exploding, and the blood where the Battle of Armageddon takes place is up to the horse's bridle. The Bible says Jesus goes down to Bosra and releases God's wrath.

## REVELATION 19:15 (NLT)

*From his mouth came a sharp sword to strike down the nations. He will rule them with an iron rod. He will release the fierce wrath of God, the Almighty, like juice flowing from a winepress.*

Jesus will walk right into the latter phase of the Second Coming. Before He gets to the Mount of Olives, Jesus will destroy the armies of the Antichrist with His Word. He slays them with the sword of His mouth. Glory! This is God finally bringing recompense to people who were haughty and attacking His kingdom.

Look now at Zechariah 14:1-7 (NLT):

*Watch, for the day of the Lord is coming when your possessions will be plundered right in front of you! I will gather all the nations to fight against Jerusalem. The city will be taken, the houses looted, and the women raped. Half the population will be taken into captivity, and the rest will be left among the ruins of the city. Then the Lord will go out to fight against those nations, as he has fought in times past. On that day his feet will stand on the Mount of Olives, east of Jerusalem. And the Mount of Olives will split apart, making a wide valley running from east to west. Half the mountain will move toward the north and half toward the south. You will flee through this valley, for it will reach across to Azal. Yes, you will flee as you did from the earthquake in the days of King Uzziah of Judah. Then the Lord my God will come, and all his holy ones with him. On that day the sources of light will no longer shine, yet there will be continuous day! Only the Lord knows how this could happen. There will be no normal day and night, for at evening time it will still be light.*

Zechariah is physically showing you what will happen when Jesus sets foot on that mountain, and he throws in a number of other details. Bottom line, the Second Coming changes everything. The changes are literally day and night different. In fact, there won't be day or night. I don't know what it will be like, but Jesus will be the only light and the only light needed. He is so bright that there will be no place where shadows can exist. Just imagine Jesus being so radiant that He encompasses everything. Even the sun revolves around Him so brightly that a shadow cannot happen. As in the beginning, life everlasting returns to a planet that has been ruled by a dark angel named Lucifer.

When the Light returns, the earth doesn't even know how to handle it. The earth says, "We don't know whether it's day or night because Jesus' light is so encompassing it lights everything up. What's going on?" What's going on is the King of Kings and the Lord of Lords is back. Whoa!

Continue reading as Zechariah's description grows even more graphic.

# ZECHARIAH 14:12-15 (NLT)

*And the Lord will send a plague on all the nations that fought against Jerusalem. Their people will become like walking corpses, their flesh rotting away. Their eyes will rot in their sockets, and their tongues will rot in their mouths. On that day they will be terrified, stricken by the Lord with great panic. They will fight their neighbors hand to hand. Judah, too, will be fighting at Jerusalem. The wealth of all the neighboring nations will be captured—great quantities of gold and silver and fine clothing. This same plague will strike the horses, mules, camels, donkeys, and all the other animals in the enemy camps.*

These verses are pretty graphic. Imagine what it would be like to be Zechariah and see this all in a vision. We call Zechariah a minor prophet, but he was seeing some major stuff. What a depiction! Joel saw it and said, "Sound an alarm! Wake everybody up!" Joel interpreted it as the Holy Spirit being poured out on everybody, but really, he was talking about when God physically comes back to the planet.

# SYMBOLIC OF THE SECOND COMING: NOAH AND LOT

Let's retrack a bit more and pick up additional details. Look with me at Matthew chapters 24 and 25.

## MATTHEW 24:31–37

*And he shall send his angels with a great sound of a trumpet, and they shall gather together his elect from the four winds, from one end of heaven to the other. Now learn a parable of the fig tree; When his branch is yet tender, and putteth forth leaves, ye know that summer is nigh: so likewise ye, when ye shall see all these things, know that it is near, even at the doors. Verily I say unto you, This generation shall not pass, till all these things be fulfilled. Heaven and earth shall pass away, but my words shall not pass away. But of that day and hour knoweth no man, no, not the angels of heaven, but my Father only. But*

**as the days of Noah were, so shall also the coming of the Son of man be.**

Jesus is speaking in a parable to His disciples. Notice verse 37 in particular. I like the parallels that Jesus gives us. For example, what happened to Noah? He went through the flood—actually, he rode on top of it. Elsewhere in the Bible, Jesus compares the Second Coming to the days of Lot. What happened to Lot? He escaped judgment. The angel said to Lot, "I can't do anything until I get you out of the city."

In both these types or symbolic representations—Noah and Lot—Jesus is giving you two thought patterns for the Church. Noah didn't get hurt, and Lot escaped. In other words, Jesus is telling us the Church escapes, and the Jews will go through the flood.

Let's look further along in Matthew 24:38-41:

*For as in the days that were before the flood they were eating and drinking, marrying and giving in marriage, until the day that Noe entered into the ark, and knew not until the*

*flood came, and took them all away; so shall*
*also the coming of the Son of man be. Then*
*shall two be in the field; the one shall be*
*taken, and the other left. Two women shall be*
*grinding at the mill; the one shall be taken,*
*and the other left.*

Now remember, Jesus is not talking about the
Rapture here as people often misconstrue; He's
talking about the Second Coming.

I was preaching in France a while back, and
we talked about this. In France, one percent of the
population is saved. In Germany, three percent is
saved. Still, from the scripture we read, that ulti-
mately there will be revival where about 50 percent get saved. It's just unacceptable to me that a
nation could have only one or three percent born
again. Then again, during the end times even sign
after sign after sign after pressure after seal after
trumpet judgment after vial judgment, only half
the people turn to God. You would think the per-
centage would be totally different as people think,
*Man, I've never seen fireworks like this in all my life.*

*I better repent!* It's absolutely absurd that the other half is saying, "It's not worth it to repent."

Nevertheless, Jesus removes the unrighteous off the earth and leaves the righteous. Again, this text does not refer to the Rapture but the Second Coming. In fact, all the accounts in Matthew refer to the Second Coming, even though I hear preachers all over the world mistakenly explain it otherwise. Jesus is very, very clear in Matthew 24.

# SHEEP AND GOAT JUDGMENT

In Matthew 25, we read more about Jesus sitting on the throne of His kingdom, and the Sheep and Goat Judgment or "the Judgment of the Nations."

## MATTHEW 25:31-34

*When the Son of man shall come in his glory, and all the holy angels with him, then shall he sit upon the throne of his glory: And before him shall be gathered all nations: and he shall separate them one from another, as a shepherd*

*divideth his sheep from the goats: And he shall*
*set the sheep on his right hand, but the goats on*
*the left. Then shall the King say unto them on*
*his right hand, Come, ye blessed of my Father,*
*inherit the kingdom prepared for you from the*
*foundation of the world.*

Notice it doesn't say in verse 31 when Jesus comes back to catch the Church away and receive it unto Himself. No. That's a whole different event that was seven years earlier. At the Rapture we go up to meet Jesus in the air. At the Second Coming, Jesus physically comes back and puts His foot on the Mount of Olives. These are two completely and totally separate events.

These scriptures above speak of the Second Coming when Jesus wants natural-bodied, righteous people to "inherit the kingdom prepared for you from the foundation of the world." When Adam sinned, Jesus didn't say, "Oops. He messed up. Too bad. It won't happen now." No, it was simply an interruption in God's plan. Yet, right here, Jesus is returning to God's plan. Even though they're not glorious like Adam and Eve were before the Fall,

He likes a natural kingdom, a natural earth. Too often people have this weird thinking that heaven is ethereal, but the truth is, heaven is more real than the earth.

God wants natural man to have a natural kingdom, and He's going to reign in that natural kingdom for a thousand years. Jesus will reign on David's throne. Talk about humility—Jesus will sit on a man's throne. I believe that Jesus' humility will be the one thing that shocks us the most when we see Him face to face. His mercy, kindness, and humility will impact you unbelievably.

There's a lot of erroneous teaching about the Sheep and Goat Judgment because people misunderstand who Jesus is talking to and what He means in Matthew 7.

## MATTHEW 7:21-23 (NLT)

*Not everyone who calls out to me, "Lord! Lord!" will enter the Kingdom of Heaven. Only those who actually do the will of my Father in heaven will enter. On judgment day many will say to me, "Lord! Lord! We prophesied in your name and cast out demons in your name and*

*performed many miracles in your name."But I*
*will reply, "I never knew you. Get away from*
*me, you who break God's laws."*

On Judgment Day people say to Jesus, "Lord!
Lord! We prophesied in Your name, cast out
demons in Your name, and performed miracles in
Your name." Jesus responds, "I never knew you.
Get away from Me." That is not Jesus talking to
the Church. It refers to people in the latter part of
the Tribulation who try to work their way into the
Second Coming. Sadly, people misdirect the whole
passage by directing this scene toward the Church
to scare people into salvation. It's disgusting to pro-
mote fear in people.

You will see here that Jesus judges the nations
based on how they treat Israel during that time. I
believe Iran and Iraq probably won't be here, but
there will be people from those nations who are
there. A nation as a whole that doesn't treat Israel
correctly will not enter the Millennial Kingdom.

Egypt will be there, although over the years
Egypt has been horrible to Israel. But one president of Egypt, Anwar Sadaat, made peace with

Israel, and it blesses the whole nation for a thousand years. He paid a price for it. His plan was to be a friend to Israel, but he was assassinated. He was shot during a parade the day after he made peace with Israel.

# GOD'S KINGDOM

God's kingdom is a very physical thing. You will notice that the land will be partitioned based on tribe—Tribe of Judah, Tribe of Benjamin. The whole land will be opened and be much larger than Israel is today.

Someone might ask, "Aren't some of the wars that are happening in the Middle East kind of Israel's fault because they took the land?" No. Israel received its land by proclamation in the Balfour Declaration. Chaim Weizmann invented a way of producing acetone that helped England win World War I.[1] England was so grateful, they asked him what he wanted as a reward. He said, "I want a homeland for my people." So, the Balfour Declaration was a public statement issued by the British government in 1917 during the World War

I, announcing a "national home for the Jewish people" in Palestine, which was then an Ottoman region with a small minority of Jewish people.

Through the United Nations, U.S. President Harry Truman put forth the very first vote to pass a declaration saying Israel had a right to their land because they were there thousands of years before. So, let's be clear. Every war from then until now is not because Palestine is defending their nation from Israel who took their land. Israel didn't take anything. Their nation was to them by proclamation of God, England, and the United States.

People often say, "But Israel is occupying Palestinian land." Wrong. They are not "occupying" anything. It's theirs!

It would be like someone from Canada coming to America and saying, "We're taking Colorado."

"No, you're not taking Colorado. It's part of the U.S.A.," you would respond.

"You're occupying Colorado."

"Well, you're not occupying Colorado."

Wouldn't that be crazy? It makes no sense whatsoever. When it comes to Israel, Lucifer has deceived the whole world into thinking Israel is to blame for war in the Middle East. The Palestinians continually stab, bomb, and aggressively and violently attack Israel. Jews must be continually on guard against these acts of violence round the clock. We have no conception of this kind of Luciferic mentality the Jews encounter on a daily basis.

But what we do know is that you and I will have a front-row seat for the battle of the ages. A rebel angel named Lucifer dared say, "I'll be like the Most High." After a six-day period when the angel tried to destroy God's creation, God said, "No you won't. I'll send the seed that will bruise you." Hallelujah. And Jesus came and redeemed us from Adam's fall, and this whole plan is playing out while we're alive on the earth.

> But what we do know is that you and I will have a front-row seat for the battle of the ages.

If you were here 500 years ago, you would say, "Wow. Well, I have no idea what's going on." But you are watching the battle of the ages unfold where Lucifer is saying, "I'm going to kill Israel." He can't get to the Father, so He tries to get what's on the Father's heart. He wants to annihilate them. But the devil cannot kill Israel. He's tried, but he just can't get it done. In the midst of it all, God raised up the Church, so for the past 2,000-year period God has had the believer on earth with the keys to the kingdom. Come on now!

During the Millennium, God will tout you and show you off. It's amazing how He will brag on His kids who first trusted in Him. God will show forth His glory because you trusted in Him when you couldn't see Him. He's proud of you, believer!

Amazingly enough, however, Jesus will reign right here on earth for a thousand years, and people still will reject Him. Not you—you trusted Him when some guy preached the Bible, so God will say, "Look at my Church. They took Me at My Word." *Wow.*

We are viewing this battle unfold right this minute, and right after we exit the planet via the Rapture, God will physically deal with Lucifer. He defeated him 2,000 years ago, and the bully has been under our feet ever since. But it won't be long before Jesus tosses him in a deep dark pit.

# PHYSICAL CHANGES

The Sheep and Goat Judgment happens immediately, but after that, there's not a lot written about the physical changes implemented as the Millennial Reign begins. The Bible talks about a 75-day interval period, and there's about 25 days for something else to happen.

There's also about 45 days to cleanse the Temple that will be rebuilt. For God to be here, even the dirt has to go through natural purifications. Even the dirt has to get ready for Him to come back. There will be 45 days of physical purification to get ready for God to be there. There will still be natural people there who have the stain of Adam on them, and God's like, "I can't have that stain near Me." Think about it. The Temple area has to be cleaned for 45 days, and yet, God lives in you. Whoooo! He who knew no sin was made sin that I'd be made the righteousness of God in Him (2 Cor. 5:21). He didn't deserve sin, but He was made sin. I didn't deserve righteousness, but He made me righteous. This gives you a picture of what He thinks about you.

The book of Ezekiel spends four to eight chapters discussing the particulars of the Temple where Jesus will dwell. There are all kinds of natural and spiritual things that he outlines.

Above it all, you will see Jesus smile like you've never seen before. He will say, "I get to come back, but I won't have to get beat up this time!" He's so normal. He'll be thinking, *Isn't this cool? I get to come back as proper as it ought to be.* The first time He came, He realized, *I am separated from My Father.* But this time, Jesus will say, "At last, all creation will see what My Dad is really like. I'll be able to implement the mercy of My Father for a thousand years."

Jesus raised you up to help Him implement that mercy, which is the whole point during that thousand years. Mercy will reign. Kindness will reign. Goodness will reign. We are all in preparation for implementing that thousand-year kingdom.

Jesus, we bow our hearts in adoration to You even now. We recognize that the earth is just about to prepare for all these traumatic events, but we are so thankful and blessed that we get to focus on the Reward Seat of Christ and the Marriage Supper of the Lamb. We get to focus on this grand event where You physically return to be seen by all and receive the honor due Your name. Every knee will bow, every tongue will confess and bless Your wonderful name, dear Jesus. Honor and dominion and power unto You who was and is and is to come. Hallelujah.

It's been said that the book of Revelation is a book of worship because the entire book is about Jesus being revealed and how we worship Him as King. The book is also about His love for us and His return for us. The Lord prompts me over and over and over to make sure His people know how much He loves them.

The purpose of end-time teaching is to convey to *you* how excited Jesus is to see *you*, and He wants you excited to see Him as well.

> **The purpose of end-time teaching is to convey to *you* how excited Jesus is to see *you*, and He wants you excited to see Him as well.**

Think how much you love some of the people in your life. That's only a fraction of His love for you. You can multiply that many times over, and you still wouldn't be able to wrap your head around His great love for you. But God is planning to express that love to bless you throughout eternity. What He has planned for you is beyond amazing.

# CHAPTER 4

# IT'S TIME TO HUSTLE

Before long, there's coming a day when you will hear a trumpet blast to end all blasts and, in the time it takes to blink your eyes, you will be changed to meet Jesus in the air. Death will be swallowed in triumphant life! The plan of God will consummate in the Rapture to finish off the Church Age. What a day to live! We ought to be able to follow you around and write down the signs and wonders the Lord is doing in your life as you write your own chapter in the book of Acts and fill out your resume for the Millennium.

The apostle Paul had something to say about this day in 1 Corinthians 15:51-54, 58 (TLB):

*I am telling you this strange and wonderful secret: we shall not all die, but we shall all* *be given new bodies! It will all happen in a moment, in the twinkling of an eye, when the last trumpet is blown. For there will be a trumpet blast from the sky, and all the Christians who have died will suddenly become alive, with new bodies that will never, never die; and then we who are still alive shall suddenly have new bodies too. For our earthly bodies, the ones we have now that can die, must be transformed into heavenly bodies that cannot perish but will live forever. When this happens, then at last this Scripture will come true—"Death is swallowed up in victory." ...So, my dear brothers, since future victory is sure, **be strong and steady, always abounding in the Lord's work, for you know that nothing you do for the Lord is ever wasted as it would be if there were no resurrection.**

The Message translation puts verse 58 this way, "With all this going for us, my dear, dear friends, *stand your ground. And don't hold back. Throw yourselves into the work of the Master....*"

That's the whole point right there. Don't hold back! It's time to throw yourself into the work of the Master. Church, it's time to *hustle!*

# FINISH OFF THE CHURCH AGE

We have just a little time left and a great destiny to finish off the Church Age in book of Acts style. When I say a little bit of time, I mean there "ain't much." So, let's have an explosion of salvations, healings, and miracles before we exit the planet. Let's take as many people to heaven as we can. Let's let the world know that Jesus is King of Kings, and He's coming soon.

> So, let's have an explosion of salvations, healings, and miracles before we exit the planet. Let's take as many people to heaven as we can.

This is such good news for the Christian, but it's a downright scary time for the world. I would not want to be living without God anytime but especially in the days to come. With everything happening now and everything yet ahead, I would be like, "Dear Jesus! I'm going to dig a hole and climb in."

Don't misunderstand me. The world is not coming to an end; Jesus is coming back to save the world. He will stop war at the Second Coming. Planet Earth will be renovated—not demolished but improved and enhanced. This earth will be here forever. You have God's word on it! Speaking of the rainbow in Genesis 9:12, "God said, "This is the sign of the covenant which I make between Me and you, and every living creature that is with you, *for perpetual generations*" (NKJV).

But the Church Age is coming to an end, and you must know all about it. In fact, there are two things God tells us not to be misinformed about: the gifts of the Spirit and the coming of the Lord. On both topics, the Lord wants you spiritually accurate and acute so you can be used by Him.

## EPHESIANS 6:10 (MSG)

*And that about wraps it up. God is strong, and he wants you strong. So take everything the Master has set out for you, well-made weapons of the best materials. And put them to use so you will be able to stand up to everything the Devil throws your way. This is no weekend war that we'll walk away from and forget about in a couple of hours. This is for keeps, a life-or-death fight to the finish against the Devil and all his angels.*

Listen, God told you to be strong in *His mighty power!* (See Ephesians 6:10 TLB.) That means as we hustle to finish off the age, we can expect the absolute wildest, most unexpected victories before Jesus comes. You and I will see out-of-the-box, unusual, radical, supernatural, scriptural signs, wonders, and miracles.

# HOW TO HUSTLE

The apostle Paul knew all about hustling, and here's what he told Titus on the topic.

## TITUS 2:12-15 (VOICE)

*…Run away from anything that leads us away from God; abandon the lusts and passions of this world; live life now in this age with **awareness** and self-control, doing the right thing and keeping yourselves holy. **Watch for His return;** expect the blessed **hope we all will share** when our great God and Savior, Jesus the Anointed, appears again. He gave His body for our sakes and will not only break us free from the chains of wickedness, but He will also prepare a community uncorrupted by the world that He would call His own—people who are passionate about doing the right thing.*

The King James Version says in verse 14 that Jesus redeemed a "peculiar people, zealous of good works." Right now is the season for zealous good works. That's why the Lord expects us to hustle for Him. You and I are the last runners of the race, so Jesus expects more push out of us. We're blessed and privileged, and we ought to act like it.

> You and I are the last runners of the race, so Jesus expects more push out of us. We're blessed and privileged, and we ought to act like it.

# JESUS FIRST

Jesus is well aware that we are so near to stepping into eternity that we cannot afford to put anything ahead of what He's telling us to do. Jesus wants you to enjoy life, sports, and hobbies, but if they are all you think about then something is not right. Jesus doesn't want you to put anything before your call or your assignment or whatever He may tell you to do.

For example, I love golf. I even ask the Lord to help me with my golf swing, and He does. I'll get up to make a shot and say, "Okay, Lord, You'll have to fix this."

He'll say, "Tuck your right elbow." He helps me every time I play golf. But if I got up to preach and was thinking about my golf swing, something would be terribly out of order. Like I said, I love golf, but I love Jesus way more. He is way more important than golf.

Why am I going through all this in a book on end times? Because we don't have much time before the Head of the Church leans over the banister of heaven on His way down and yells, "Come up hither! Come up to the throne of God!" I want to make sure that with the time we have left, we are not focused on the wrong things or whatever your hobby is. Keep your priorities straight. Too many people don't have time to go to church because they are so busy with activities. How close do we have to get to the Rapture before we make some changes in our lives?

The payoff is just over the top in the Millennial Reign of Christ. Then, you can have all the hobbies you want—learn to play instruments, ski, golf, whatever. A billion years from now, you'll have all the toys you want. But get this—eternity is coming. Play then. Hustle for Jesus now.

Jesus is trying to warn you: "Time is short!" It's not a bad warning. It's a wonderful warning because He wants to adorn you with medals at the

Reward Seat of Christ. Wouldn't it be cool afterward to say to those around you, "Check this out!" with your medals glowing.

People will look at you and say to each other, "Wow, did you see all that gold and silver? That person was wholehearted. That person gave Jesus his all. Jesus adorned her faithfulness, and she will wear it forever." We will thump each other during the Millennium and point out different ones. "Wow! That's awesome. That person really made his or her life count!" Make your life count so you have an abundant entrance into heaven. Recognize the importance of the hour and ask Jesus how you can run your race faster. Ask Him where and how He wants you to serve Him. And, above all, put Jesus first!

# THE FIRST STEP TO
# FOREVER WITH JESUS!

To meet Jesus in the air when the trumpet blasts at the Rapture and return with Jesus at the Second Coming to live with Him forever, there's one important thing you must do. You must receive Jesus Christ as your Savior and Lord. It's the most important decision you'll ever make, and it's as easy as believing and praying the prayer below aloud.

> *Dear heavenly Father:*
> *Your Word says, "Whosoever shall call on the name of the Lord shall be saved" (Acts 2:21). I call on You right now!*
>
> *The Bible says if I confess with my mouth that Jesus is Lord and believe in my heart that You have raised Him from the dead, I will be saved (Romans 10:9-10).*
>
> *Jesus, I believe in my heart and confess*

*with my mouth that You were raised from the dead. I ask You now to be my Savior and Lord. Thank You for forgiving me of sin.*

*Second Corinthians 5:17 says this means I now belong to You and have become a new person on the inside. The old life is gone; a new life has begun in Jesus' name. Amen.*

If you have just prayed this prayer, please share your good news with us at office@josephmorris .com.

# NOTES

**Chapter 2 // The Rapture**

1. Strong's #726: harpazo (pronounced har-pad'-zo) from a derivative of 138; to seize (in various applications): catch (away, up), pluck, pull, take (by force). Thayer's Greek Lexicon: harpazō: to snatch out or away.

**Chapter 3 // The Second Coming of Jesus**

1. Michael Freemantle, "The Weizmann Contribution," ChemistryWorld, July 5, 2017, https://www.chemistryworld.com/opinion/the-weizmann-contribution/3007435.article.

From
# Joseph Morris

### 75+ Signs of Jesus' Soon Return!

As the world grows more volatile with looming wars, rampant pandemics, and violence in the streets, many people are wondering, *Is the end near?*

YES! Jesus is coming soon! But it's wonderful news!

There is also plenty of bad news on the horizon—but not for the Christian. Jesus' end-time agenda is to give you great hope and joy. He wants to bless you and prepare you for your destiny in these last days.

For more than 30 years, author, minister, and host of the weekly *End of Days Update*, Joseph Morris has been awakening the Church to Jesus' hastening return, helping believers connect the dots between Bible prophecy and current events.

In *End Times Made Easy*, Joseph shares:

- Scriptural evidence of end-time events happening right now
- Easy-to-understand charts
- The difference between the Rapture and the Second Coming
- Answers to tough questions about the Tribulation
- Amazing biblical descriptions of Jesus' millennial reign on earth

The simple truths in this book will empower you to run your race with joy in these last days excited to see Jesus face to face!

## Purchase your copy wherever books are sold.

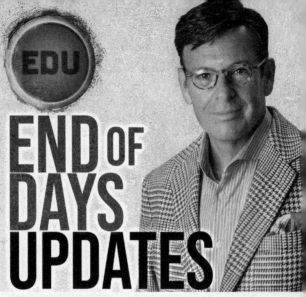

# EDU

# END OF DAYS UPDATES

Weekly updates
where Bible prophecy
meets headline news...
UNTIL JESUS RETURNS!

SUBSCRIBE NOW ON YOUTUBE / EDU / JOSEPH MORRIS MINISTRIES